BOWLING BASICS

by
Chuck Pezzano

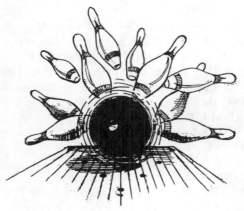

Illustrated by
Bill Gow

With Photographs

Created and Produced by
Arvid Knudsen

Prentice-Hall, Inc.
Englewood Cliffs, New Jersey

Dedicated to Lila, with love.

Acknowledgment

My thanks go to the American Bowling Congress, Dr. George Allen, AMF, Brunswick Corporation, the National Bowling Council, the Professional Bowlers Association, Bill Taylor, the Women's International Bowling Congress, and the Young American Bowling Alliance for their guidance, information, and photos.

Other Sports Basics Books in Series

Text copyright © 1984 by Chuck Pezzano and Arvid Knudsen
Illustrations copyright © 1984 by Arvid Knudsen

Printed in the United States of America   · J

Prentice-Hall International, Inc., London
Prentice-Hall of Australia, Pty. Ltd., Sydney
Prentice-Hall of Canada, Inc., Toronto
Prentice-Hall of India Private Ltd., New Delhi
Prentice-Hall of Japan, Inc., Tokyo
Prentice-Hall of Southeast Asia Pte. Ltd., Singapore
Whitehall Books Limited, Wellington, New Zealand
Editora Prentice-Hall do Brasil Ltda., Rio de Janeiro

10 9 8 7 6 5 4 3 2 1

Library of Congress Cataloging in Publication Data

Pezzano, Chuck.
  Bowling basics.

  Includes index.
  Summary: An introduction to the techniques, rules, equipment and competitions of bowling.
  1. Bowling—Juvenile literature. [1. Bowling]
I. Gow, Bill, ill. II. Knudsen, Arvid. III. Title.
GV902.5.P48   1984   794.6   83-22893
ISBN 0-13-080516-5   (Rev.)

CONTENTS

A SHORT HISTORY OF BOWLING

The odds are that as long as man has been around, so has some form of bowling.

Cave men, despite their primitive state, were forced to perfect simple hunting skills. Since their basic weapons were crude spears or loose stones, they practiced for the life-saving hunt by throwing stones at targets.

One of the broad appeals of bowling is a natural tendency to gain some sort of satisfaction from throwing things at other things, either to amaze by showing off skill, amuse by the fun of it all, or relieve by using the exertion to diminish mental or physical pressures and emotions.

Implements for games similar to bowling have been unearthed in and near Egyptian grave sites, some as many as 7,000 years old. Many have been discovered in the tombs of children. The logical conclusion is that bowling equipment was added to amuse the departed in the next world.

As time went on, just about every country developed its own form of bowling, each deciding on its own type of ball, pins, lanes, and courts, in various shapes and sizes.

Bocci (spelled many different ways), an Italian form of the game still played on carefully maintained courts throughout the United States, got its start at the time of Julius Caesar, about 75 B.C.

Another word for bowler is *kegler*, taken from the German. In the early Christian days in Germany, many people carried a stick or club shaped somewhat like a crude pin. It was called a *kegle* or *kegel*, and it was used as a cane or even as a weapon.

But it also had a religious meaning. A person suspected of not following church rules was asked to set up his *kegle* as a pin. Then he was given a stone to try to knock it down, as it represented the Devil. If he knocked it down, he was living right. If not, he was advised to mend his ways. Participants became known as *keglers*, a word still used everywhere to denote bowlers.

And so it went, from hazy and disorganized beginnings throughout the world, to the highly sophisticated sport we now know as American Tenpins. Today, the sport is played competitively in more than seventy countries.

Bowling was first brought to this country by the Dutch, so from the early 1600s bowling enjoyed popularity. Bowling had its ups and downs because it often led to gambling and because it lacked effective organization. In the early days, men did most of the bowling, and most of it was done in cellars or basements or in a place that was part of a saloon.

In the late 1800s bowling began to come into its own, and much of the bowling was conducted in club or church lanes with the approval and support of those organizations. But the sport still lacked a central governing organization, and so the type of lanes, bowling balls, pins, and rules varied according to where you rolled, who was in charge in that area, and how much attention was given to enforcement. The various leaders knew that growth was impossible in such a situation.

So in 1895, with representatives from all groups, an historic meeting in New York City resulted in the formation of the American Bowling Congress (ABC). Among those gathered were the finest minds in the sport, and time has proven their knowledge and wisdom. Most of the rules and specifications for both lane and personal equipment remain little changed almost a century later.

The American Bowling Congress has continued as a nonprofit organization of male tenpin bowlers dedicated to the establishment of playing rules, equipment standards, and the promotion of bowling as recreation and as a competitive sport. Women bowlers organized in 1916 to form the Women's International Bowling Congress (WIBC).

Today there are more than 5,000 local ABC and WIBC associations manned by more than 100,000 volunteer workers who keep the rules of the game well defined for all. Bowling is the same everywhere in the world as long as it has the approval of the ABC or the WIBC. And at any time of the day or night, someone somewhere is bowling in a league or tournament. There are 10 million men, women, and children who roll in league play, and in any given year, more than 70 million people will roll a game or two.

Young people always bowled, but in loose groups, and under tangles of local laws. In some states you had to be sixteen or eighteen before you could step into a bowling center. In others you couldn't bowl unless you were with a parent or an adult to supervise you.

Organized junior bowling started back in 1936. Milt Raymer, a high school teacher in Chicago, felt that it was time to organize the way young people bowled. He put his organizational genius to work and is rightfully known as the father of the American Junior Bowling Congress. His work earned him election to the ABC Hall of Fame.

The Junior Congress had branches in every section, with the blessing and full support of the ABC and the WIBC. The bowling proprietors of the country also had a junior bowling program.

In 1982 came a unification of the junior groups to form the Young American Bowling Alliance (YABA). It covers every phase of youth bowling from start through college.

All members of the bowling family are vitally interested in youth bowling, and there are instructional clinics staged regularly. The staff at bowling headquarters are eager to help any junior bowler from the ages of two to twenty-two. There are special rule books and special award programs, and many a junior bowler has won more than one hundred awards in a short career for everything from high scores to converting splits to perfect attendance to serving as a league official.

For full information on any aspect of youth bowling, write to: Young American Bowling Alliance, 5301 South 76th Street, Greendale, Wisconsin 53129.

2 | THE BOWLING CENTER: YOUR OWN STADIUM

Bowling centers are unique in that they are all different, and yet all the same.

They range from simple two-laners in a church or club recreation area to as many as 112 lanes in a row. Some are simply constructed, others ornate with such added extras as waterfalls, full locker rooms, and gyms.

But always remember that whenever you step on the approach to roll a ball you could well be using more than $50,000 worth of equipment packaged in that single lane.

The lane is the playing surface. It stretches 62 feet, 10¾ inches from foul line to pit. The *foul line* is the black divider between the approach, the area the player uses to get to the foul line, and the actual surface where the ball makes contact with the lane and rolls on down. The pit is the area where the ball winds up after going through the pins.

It is 60 feet from the foul line to the center of the headpin. The *pin deck* is the area where the pins are set. The pins are placed on pin spots, which are clearly stamped or printed, 2¼ inches in diameeter and 12 inches from center to center of adjacent pin spots. The pin spots are arranged in a 36-inch triangle.

The playing portion of the lane is 41½ inches wide with a tolerance of ½ inch, so a lane can be between 41 and 42 inches. The channels on each side add 9¼ to 9⅜ inches for an overall width of 60 to 60¼ inches.

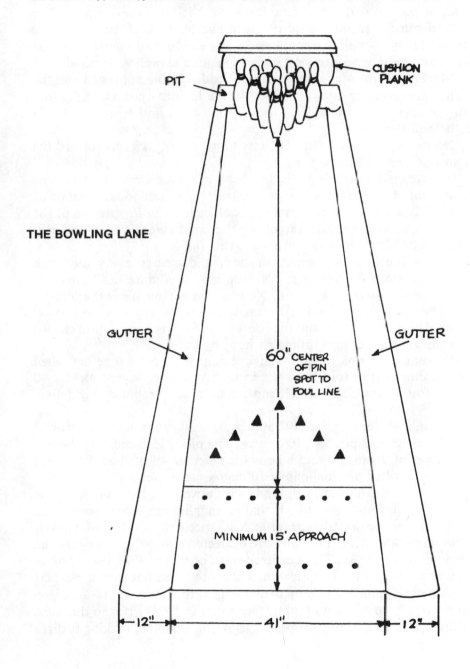

THE BOWLING LANE

CUSHION PLANK

PIT

GUTTER

GUTTER

60" CENTER OF PIN SPOT TO FOUL LINE

MINIMUM 15' APPROACH

12" — 41" — 12"

The approach must be at least 15 feet long. Most are 16 feet long. The approach and first portion of the playing surface are constructed of hard wood, most often hard rock maple. Then from there to the pin deck the wood is pine, a softer wood, and the pin deck is usually maple. The harder and sturdier wood is used up front and in the back because those are the two areas taking the most physical abuse. More and more synthetic materials are being used as wood becomes scarce as well as expensive.

Markings, dots and arrows, are embedded in the approach and the lane. They are targeting devices, located at the 15-foot mark from the foul line on the approach, and also at the 12-foot mark and from two to six inches behind the line.

On the lane, beyond the foul line, targets are 6 to 8 feet toward the pins and also from 12 to 16 feet.

The targets must be equidistant and set in a uniform pattern. They are at five board intervals. A lane is constructed of individual sections of wood called boards, each approximately one inch wide. Proper use of the dots on the approach with the targets on the lanes gives bowlers an accurate method of planning a shot from start to finish.

A bowling lane is cleaned, dressed, and treated every day with various applications of lane coatings, lacquers, urethanes, and oils. For many years it was all done by hand. Now automatic machines that can be set as to the amount of covering are used. The coating is used to protect the wood, which could not stand the constant pounding and friction caused by the constant impact and rolling of bowling balls.

Bowling pins look rather small and bunched closely together when you're standing at the foul line, but in reality they represent almost 40 pounds of tough wood and plastic more than able to repulse and deflect the ball.

A pin, in order to gain ABC approval, must range in weight from 3 pounds, 6 ounces to 3 pounds, 10 ounces. The pin is 15 inches high with a base diameter of 2¼ inches and a belly diameter of 4¾ inches. A pin will fall if it can be tilted approximately 10 degrees to either side.

Though most pins are still made with a wooden base and a plastic outer coating, various materials, including magnesium, have been used, and development continues constantly. ABC specifications for all types of lane equipment are strict, and lanes are inspected regularly to see that the standards are maintained. The lane itself must be within 40/1,000ths of an inch in levelness and depth depression. That's about as flat as you can get!

One development in equipment changed the entire sport—the successful introduction of the automatic pinspotter in 1952. Prior to that time a bowling center had to rely on people to set up the pins, making it diffi-

THE PIN

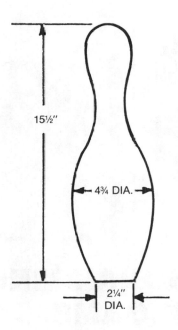

15½"

4¾ DIA.

2¼" DIA.

cult to maintain huge centers at all hours of the day or night. The machines that took over this task gave rise to the large, modern, plush centers of today, many of which are open twenty-four hours a day.

AMF and Brunswick are the manufacturers of mechanical bowling equipment, and each year the machinery becomes easier to work with and more trouble free. The latest innovation in bowling is automatic scoring. These amazing additions to the sport keep score for individuals and teams, can handle handicaps, and supply readout sheets.

The evolution of the sport has been steady, and rules, regulations, and equipment have been geared to create and maintain a challenging, yet not discouraging, competitive sport.

When you go into a bowling center, don't be afraid to ask questions of the people there. The control desk is the center of the operation. Though there is no great mystery in handling whatever is necessary, don't hesitate to ask how something works.

Treat all the equipment you use with the same delicate respect you would give to your most treasured possessions.

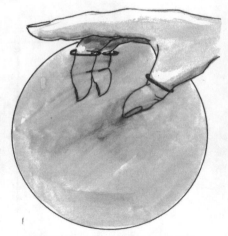

1) CONVENTIONAL FIT: FINGERS
INSERTED TO SECOND JOINT

3 | PERSONALIZING YOUR GAME

All an aspiring bowler needs in order to roll is a bowling ball and bowling shoes. Both are readily available at any bowling center.

Bowling balls come in assorted weights, colors, and balances. They are made of various materials, such as rubber, plastic, and even some secret combinations. The science of bowling ball drilling has become very sophisticated, and any young bowler should rely on a professional ball driller to meet his or her needs.

You should know that a bowling ball cannot exceed sixteen pounds in weight and must conform to a consistent balance on the top, bottom, and sides. The weight is the first factor for young bowlers to consider. There are bowling balls as light as eight pounds, but you should use the weight you can handle. If the ball feels too heavy or seems to throw you, then drop down to a lighter weight.

Remember, bowling is more a sport of timing and coordination than one of strength, and comfort and naturalness should come first.

After weight, the span is most important. The *span* is the distance from the inside edge of the thumb hole to the inside edge of the finger holes. A span too narrow can cause strain on the fingers, thumb, wrist, or arm.

To determine the proper span for a conventional grip, place the thumb all the way into the thumb hole. The fit should be loose enough to allow rotation with only minor friction.

2) SEMI-FINGERTIP FIT:
FINGERS INVERTED BETWEEN
1ST AND 2ND JOINT.

3) FINGERTIP FIT: FINGERS
INSERTED TO FIRST JOINT.

Then the two middle fingers should be stretched over (not into) the finger holes. The bend of the second joint should extend about one-quarter inch beyond the inner edge of the finger holes. Human skin varies. Some is stiff, some very elastic. Allow tolerance for your type.

In simple terms, if the finger bends don't reach the edge, the span is too wide. If they go too far past the quarter- to half-inch area, the span is too narrow.

The three basic types of grip are the previously mentioned conventional grip, the wide conventional (also referred to as a *semi-fingertip grip*), and the fingertip grip.

The fingertip grip is drilled so that the span is so wide that the bowler can insert fingers only to the first joint or bend. This grip is normally used by more advanced bowlers who want more lift, turn, and leverage at release. This lift and turn applied at the time of release give the ball more revolutions—thus more action when the ball hits the pins.

The fingertip grip is also easier on the fingers and hand if a bowler rolls a large number of games. Although the fingertip grip was frowned on for beginners years ago, many young bowlers move right into it shortly after they learn the basics of the sport. This is an individual decision that comes with experience.

The semi-fingertip grip is a drilling that places the fingers in the holes somewhere between the conventional and the fingertip, the two extremes of grips.

Bowling ball drilling has become a science. There are many types of bowling ball surfaces, complicated weights, and grips and balances, so these decisions should be made for you by an expert.

EQUIPMENT

BALL AND BAG

SHOES

BOWLING GLOVE

TEE SHIRT OR
REGULAR SHIRT

JACKET

14

An experienced bowling pro will take a good look at a bowler, use background information and perhaps even personality as a contributing factor, and give the bowler what he or she needs.

Young bowlers should be aware that they grow quickly and should have their bowling balls checked every six months to a year so that the finger and thumb holes can be enlarged. If there is more growth and strength, of course, the bowler should switch to a heavier ball.

Bowling shoes are a must for all bowlers of all ages. They can be rented, but it is best to have your own. The custom-made, better type of shoe uses different materials on the soles of each shoe to allow gripping and sliding freedom, both necessary.

The other clothing you wear while bowling is important too. Avoid extremes. Be comfortable. Loose clothing is best, but not so loose that extra material gets in the way of proper arm, shoulder, leg, or foot movements.

There are many bowling aids on the market. These range from wristlets which firm the wrist to inserts for thumb and finger holes to give a better grip to towels for keeping your hands free of perspiration. Don't be afraid to use them if they are sold in a pro shop, but don't overdo it either. There are no magic grips or magic aids to make you a bowler overnight. Some might help, but always check to see if other bowlers use them or if a pro endorses them.

Personal bowling equipment—balls, bags, shoes, uniforms, aids— are all comparatively inexpensive, so as soon as possible try to obtain your own. It is much easier and much better for your game than renting and using different equipment each time you bowl.

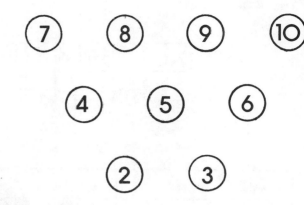

ALWAYS CALL PINS BY NUMBERS

4 KNOW HOW TO KEEP SCORE

At a baseball or football game you can't tell much without a score-card. In bowling you can't tell anything without a scoresheet. And you really don't know what is going on unless you're well versed in keeping score.

In this age of automation you can learn to bowl, actually bowl in league and tournament competition, and not know how to keep score well —or even at all. The robots and the computers do it all for you, or do they?

Pros have lost tournaments because they didn't check the score closely enough and miscalculated what they needed in the final frame or on the final ball. In many situations knowing the exact score will determine whether you will attempt to make an almost impossible split or just settle for the knockdown of one or two pins that can be made without much trouble.

As a bowler you should be able to project your own score and the score of your opponent, so that no matter what frame you're in you know what the potentials are in both cases.

Scoring in bowling is not nearly as complicated as it sometimes seems, and the more you do it, the easier it becomes. So take every opportunity to keep score—your own, your team's, and even the score at tournaments where often you might receive a small fee or some free games of bowling in return for keeping the score.

NAME	1	2	3	4	5	6	7	8	9	10
JIM	X	X	X	7 2	8 /	F 9	X	7 /	9 -	X X 8
	30	57	76	85	95	104	124	143	152	180

A game is made up of ten frames. The scoresheet will show two horizontal parallel lines divided into ten boxes. In most cases smaller boxes or squares will be located at the upper right-hand section of each large box.

In each of the first nine frames you roll one or two balls. When you knock down all ten pins with the first ball, that's the ultimate, a *strike*. That completes the frame, so there is no need to roll a second ball. If you fail to knock down all the pins with your first ball, you are allowed a second ball. If you knock down the remaining pins with your second ball you are credited with a *spare*. The pins remaining after the first ball are spare leaves.

A strike is worth ten plus the number of pins you knock down with your next two balls, so your maximum possible score in each frame is thirty pins. If you score a strike in the tenth and final frame you are granted two additional balls. If you register all strikes—nine in the first nine frames, and three in the final frame—you have a perfect game of 300, a score of thirty for each of the ten frames.

A spare is second best to a strike and means to knock all ten pins down with two balls. That gives you ten plus the number of pins you knock down with your next ball. So the most you can score in a frame in which you have a spare is twenty—ten for the spare, and ten more if you can score a strike on the next ball. When you make a spare, it is referred to as converting a spare.

If you don't knock down all ten pins with both balls, you simply record the number of pins, and that is known as a *miss* or an *error*.

Scoring markings are the same the world over. A strike is designated by an ×. A spare is registered by a /, although some people reverse the direction of the slash. A split is shown by a small circle (∘), and the miss or error is recorded with a simple horizontal line (–). The latter two markings are for informational purposes.

A *split* is defined as a spare leave remaining after the first ball has been legally delivered in which the head pin is down and at least one other pin is down between two or more other pins which remain standing. For example, the 3–10, 5–7, or 8–10. In most cases you are expected to convert spares, but splits are much more difficult, so when your game is dotted with splits, it isn't as mentally discouraging a game as one loaded with errors.

The two small boxes in the upper right corner of each larger box representing a frame are used to give a ball-by-ball count of the game. This is important if you're interested in having a complete record. It's invaluable when you want to go back to check a close game for a possible error, because you must know the number of pins knocked down by each ball.

The first ball is recorded in the first of the small boxes. If it is a strike, that's it. If the bowler does not strike, the number of pins on the first ball is entered in the box. If it is a split, the small circle goes around the first number. Either the mark representing a spare (/) or the number of pins knocked down on the second ball fills the second box.

Remember that scoring is progressive, frame by frame, and the actual score in one frame may not be determined until two frames later. This happens when a bowler racks up a string of strikes. A *double* (two strikes in a row) or a *turkey* (three strikes in a row) happily delay the scoring.

Keep thinking in tens, like ten for a strike plus pins knocked down with the next two balls or ten for a spare plus what is knocked down with the next ball.

A game may seem hopelessly lost, but a little quick figuring will show that a triple strike against three open frames can pick up more than fifty pins. Knowing the score is as important as knowing all the rules about the sport. So study the illustrations here and keep score as often as you can. When you're just watching, practice those numbers in your head.

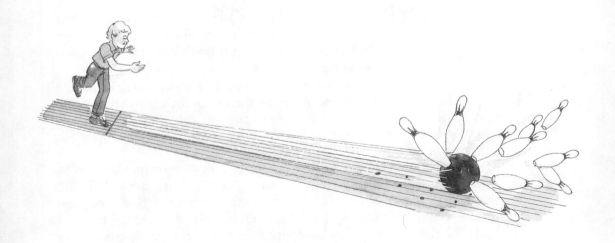

(**Note:** The instructions given are for those who are right-handed. If you're left-handed, just reverse the procedures.)

5 | THE APPROACH AND DELIVERY

The Stance

Your *stance*, or *address*, is your starting position, and this should immediately bring to mind relaxation. You will have arrived at the general position through experimentation, based on what is most comfortable for you, how many steps you take, and the size of your steps.

The four-step delivery is the basic and most recommended, so we'll discuss it in detail. If you're going to take four steps, begin at the foul line, facing *away* from the pins. Take the same type of steps you would if you had a bowling ball in your hand and were going against the pins. Take four steps, add about half a step for a slide, then turn around and look at the floor.

Check the markers (usually dots) on the approach, and take a few practice walks on the approach toward the foul line. When you are satisfied you have ascertained the proper position for you, remember where you are so that you will know where to place the toe of the foot you will use as your guide. Usually this will be the left foot in a four-step delivery.

You should be to the right of the center dot, positioned so that your arm swing will bring the ball over the second and third arrows embedded in the lane, or the tenth to fifteenth boards on the lane when you start counting from the right.

The purpose of the stance is to position the bowler so that with the least amount of effort and thinking he or she can launch the delivery and proceed smoothly and in a relaxed way to the line.

Once you decide on your point of origin, check the other important factors in your stance position:

The weight of the ball rests primarily on the nonbowling hand. The body position of the ball is based on body structure, but extremes should be avoided. Anywhere from the waist to the shoulder is fine, and well within the recommended range. The ball should be held to the right side of the body for right-handed bowlers (opposite for lefties), giving the bowler a good start on his or her straight-arm swing.

The arm should be close to the body, the wrist should be fairly firm, and the fingers should be well in the ball with the thumb inserted all the way and the thumb position at about 11 o'clock.

The shoulders should be square and parallel to the target. The eyes should be on the target.

The toes should be straight and the feet should be fairly close together, with the left foot slightly forward of the right one to give better balance and to allow the body weight to be on the left foot. The knees should be flexed slightly, more rather than less. Certainly they should not be stiff.

FOR THE STANCE, THE TOES SHOULD
BE STRAIGHT AND THE FEET SHOULD
BE FAIRLY CLOSE TOGETHER

The Pushaway

The *pushaway* is the first step of the approach, putting together the movement of the ball and the starting foot.

Push the ball forward, and at the same time move your right foot forward. The ball motion will be slightly down, and the foot movement should be slow, fairly short, and on the deliberate side. The ball should be pushed gently, and the foot should move out approximately the same distance.

Most pros consider the beginning step the most important because it sets the tone for the rest of the delivery. Any jerky or off-balance movements can magnify by the time you reach the line. Sometimes a deep breath before the first step will do much to relax your body. Exhale and then go.

Your waist and knees should be bending slightly at the end of the first step, and the nonbowling hand is still bearing much of the weight of the ball. Into the second step the nonbowling hand leaves the ball, and the bowling arm is into the free pendulum swing. The nonbowling arm moves off to add balance.

The second step brings the ball into the downswing to begin the backswing. Keep your arm as close to your body as possible, almost as a lever, to let the weight of the ball perform the straight swing. At the completion of the second step the shoulders are square to the target, the left foot is forward, and the ball should be below the shoulder, never higher. You need go back only as far as you must to maintain decent speed on the ball, but the low limit should be around the waist area.

The Backswing

The ball is at the top of the backswing when the third step is completed. The right foot is forward, the left arm is well extended, and the body is square to target. Many bowlers become anxious as they near the line, but no extra effort is needed to propel the ball.

The Slide and Ball Release

The fourth and final step is partially or fully a slide. At the beginning of this step the weight is still on your right foot, but then it shifts to the left foot, which moves into a slide. Timing is considered perfect when left foot and right arm reach the foul line at just about the same time.

In the final step, the left knee should bend and bring the body lower to give the best leverage. The left foot is fairly firmly planted, the left arm is giving you balance, and the right arm smoothly lifts the ball well over the foul line.

APPROACH AND DELIVERY

5 STEP DELIVERY

STANCE   1st Step — Left foot shuffles slightly forward.   2nd Step — Pushaway   3rd Step — Start of pendulum swing.   4th Step — Backswing.   5th Step — Ball and foot reaching foul line.   Follow-through

4 STEP DELIVERY

STANCE   1st Step — Pushaway.   2nd Step — Downswing.   3rd Step — Backswing   4th Step — Release   Follow-through

3 STEP DELIVERY

STANCE   1st Step — Pushaway, downward toward the knee.   2nd Step — Backswing   3rd Step — Ball and foot reaching foul line   Ball released over foul line.   Follow-through

24

The Follow Through

The *follow through* is the continuation of the natural arc of the swing that started way back with the pushaway. It should bring to mind extension because it is a part of your delivery. Get fully into the shot by extending the arm toward the target area. After the ball is released, your arm should flow naturally, and you should be able to remain balanced on your left foot until the ball is well underway to make contact with the pins.

Other Deliveries

Although the four-step delivery is the most popular and most recommended, the three-step and five-step are also commonly used.

The three-step is quicker all the way, and the first step must incorporate the first two steps of the four-step, calling for a more definite downward and speedier movement pushing the ball away. It takes a little more arm strength.

The five-step is essentially the same as the four-step. All you do is add another step (at the beginning) in which the ball is held. Thus, the second step of the five-step delivery is the same as the first step in the four-step delivery.

Some bowlers take as many as six or seven steps because they have a need for a faster, shorter step type of run to the line. Others take just one step by standing at the foul line, swinging the ball, then stepping forward for the ball release. This is recommended for older people and handicapped people.

Try the four-step delivery, but don't hesitate to try the five, and possibly the three. The timing is the thing no matter how many steps you take.

SPECIAL GUIDANCE FROM BILL TAYLOR

(Bill Taylor is universally recognized as one of the finest bowling instructors in the world. He has coached many of the top pro stars and has traveled to many foreign countries to set up bowling programs and conduct clinics. He prepares many young bowlers for competition in grade school, high school, college, and, some day, he hopes, the Olympics. He offers these tips specifically for young bowlers.)

Bowling is a game of targeting, and the main factors are body construction and body movements.

Your timing and your swing are the only real-problems you have to deal with right now. If you are from eight to twelve years old, you will have more trouble with the swing now than after you are older, because of the size of the ball compared with the width of your hips and shoulders. Stay with it and you will see a big difference as your shoulders broaden and your upper-body strength improves.

Timing: A bowling ball is not a baseball or football to be thrown. In order to bowl well, you must let a bowling ball swing, just like you used to swing in the playground. When you sat there and pumped the swing to go higher, you used the force of gravity, and we do the same thing with a bowling ball.

When you push the ball away from you, it wants to straighten out your arm, just like the rope or chain of the swing in the playground, and it wants to fall and swing from your shoulder like the chain swings from the bar.

And that's what you want it to do, except that you want to walk along with it, but not run. Bowling is a walk beside a swinging object. We do not run because the ball cannot freely swing that fast and keep up with the feet. That would force you to try to throw the ball, which is bad for your bowling.

How do you push? Gently. You want to push at a relaxed startup from a dead stop in the stance. Don't rush the push, and don't sneak out there ever so slowly.

Where to push? Just straight out from the shoulder while holding the ball partly over to the right almost in line with the bowling arm and shoulder. As you get older and your arms grow longer you can push down.

26

JOHN JASZKOWSKI, 11, OF SOUTH MILWAUKEE, WI, BOWLED A PERFECT
GAME ON MARCH 13, 1982. HE IS THE YOUNGEST PLAYER TO ROLL A
SANCTIONED 300 GAME.

27

When to push? Exactly when you step with the foot on the same side of your body as your bowling arm. Just start your hand and heel at the same time and try to make them arrive at the same time, with the foot solidly on the floor and the arm fully extended, ready to fall. You will get better much faster if you practice where and when to push in front of a mirror at home, about fifty times each practice session. Just take one step. You don't want to swing the ball in the house and break the mirror or some furniture!

The Approach: *Now you are in motion, and you want to stay smoothly in motion, walking wherever and whenever the swinging ball wants you to. Here is one of the tricky parts—how much to hold on to a swinging ball. You want a ball that fits so well that you do not have to squeeze real hard. Just swing it freely, and if it falls off too soon, you need a better-fitting ball. Go back to the ball driller and ask him or her to repair it.*

Your Balance Arm: *Just after you push your ball away and your arm is straightened, if your balance arm doesn't do it automatically, bring it back and point it to the left wall and leave it there until the ball is out of your hand and going down the lane. Learn to do it in a smooth, unhurried motion.*

Your Back Angle: *Don't follow the ball down with your shoulders. This is just about the worst bowling habit you could develop, and unless told not to, many youngsters do it because it seems natural to attack the pins in this forceful manner.*

Instead, think of walking tall for the first three steps, and then on your third step you relax that leg, slide, and complete the follow through straight up to the ceiling.

Your Slide and Follow Through: *The slide and follow through are easy to do when you integrate the other elements just mentioned. They are difficult to do right when you don't do your timing and swing the balance arm and back angle and relax your leg in step three right. So you want to think about pushing the ball exactly when you step. And you want to think about letting the ball fall freely while you point your balance arm and walk tall. And you want to think about them over and over again until it all comes naturally to you, like walking and eating and dressing.*

The final key thing·to learn is relaxing your leg in step three. It takes a while for the brain to tell the leg what to do in a consistent manner. Then the slide is automatic, and the follow through is automatic— nice rewards for learning the other things.

28

Targeting: *Up until the age of thirteen, try to be content to hit the headpin consistently, make spares, and get your strikes now and then. Don't frustrate yourself by trying to develop pinpoint accuracy.*

To make targeting easier keep your feet to the right and face the pins you want to hit if you are right-handed, the opposite if you are a lefty. In positioning for spares keep it simple. The farther left the spare is standing, the farther right you should stand. The farther right the spare is standing, the more to the left you should stand. Pay close attention to the dots on the approach, and remember where to stand to make certain spares (see spare-making charts and illustrations).

Warning: *If you run, try to throw the ball, bend way over, or lift the ball up high in the backswing, the chances are greater that you will not become a good bowler.*

Remember, bowling is a walk beside a freely swinging ball that fits your hand. Then it is a gradual lowering of the body by relaxing your leg in step three. The slide and follow through will then happen like magic.

Learn to do these five things well:
1. *Push the ball.*
2. *Let it fall.*
3. *Point the ball.*
4. *Walk tall.*
5. *Relax leg, step three, (Step two in three-step, step four in five-step deliveries).*

Say them as you do them, every time you bowl, and you'll bowl better and better.

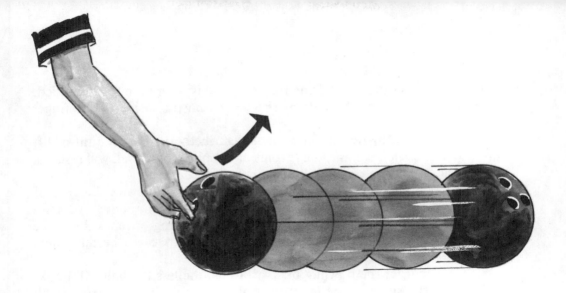

6 | TYPES OF BALLS ROLLED AND TARGETING TECHNIQUES

The position of your fingers and thumb at the split second at which you release the ball will determine what the ball will do once it starts down the lane.

Picture your bowling ball as a clock, and this will give you a good idea as to how to control the path your ball will take. In bowling there are the straight ball, hook, curve, and backup. The last is also known as a *reverse hook*.

If your thumb at the point of release is at 12 o'clock, straight toward the target, the ball will roll approximately straight.

If the thumb position is at 10 to 11 o'clock at the point of ball release, it will produce a hook ball. This is the most preferred ball to roll since it combines a ball of action with enough leeway to allow the bowler good accuracy. A hook ball moves from right to left.

The curve ball results when the thumb position is lower than 10 o'clock. The curve ball is actually a large hook.

The backup or reverse hook occurs when a ball has been released with the thumb at the 1 to 2 o'clock position. This is a clockwise spin—as opposed to the hooks, where the spin is counter-clockwise.

It is good to know what happens at the crucial point of ball release. The thumb leaves the ball first, and at that point—only a split second—the ball is resting on the flats of the fingers. Here is where the lift is applied. The *lift* is the feel of the flats of the fingers on the inside of the finger holes.

Based on the thumb position as described, and the amount of lift applied at the release point, the revolutions applied to the ball will result in a straight ball, large or small hook, or the backup.

A contributing factor will be the lane conditions and the type of bowling ball used. Too much lane dressing (oil and compounds) will tend to lessen the hooking action of the ball. Less dressing or lanes that have had excessive play on them will cause the ball to hook easier because there is more friction.

The harder the bowling ball surface is, the less the ball will hook. The softer the surface, the more the ball will hook. Today there are all types of bowling ball surfaces specifically designed for various types of lanes.

Trial-and-error quickly tells you whether the lanes are hooking or not. You can also control hooking by moving to the inside or center of the lane if you want less hook or to the outside or more toward the channel for more hook.

Targeting Techniques

The series of dots on the approach and the arrows embedded in the lane are there, as mentioned previously, to make it easier to knock down the pins.

Spot bowling (rolling over the arrows on the lane) is considered the most effective way to target. It is based on the simple theory that it is much easier to hit a spot twelve to fifteen feet away than it is to hit a spot some sixty feet down the lane. The target arrow on the lane can be used as your guide to the pocket. The pocket, or strike zone, is the 1–3 for righthanders, 1–2 for lefties. It is the area of the lane where your ball must make contact with the pins to give you the best chance to knock all ten pins down.

If your approach, angle, and ball speed are the same, and you hit the spot, your ball will end up in the 1–3 or strike pocket area.

It isn't always necessary to spot out as far as the arrows. If you prefer to look closer, just back up your line from the arrow back and select a spot along the board. Some bowlers spot just at or just beyond the foul line.

Pin bowling is the exact opposite of spot bowling. The bowler looks at the pins, keeping his or her eye on the 1–3 pocket, and attempts to guide the ball there.

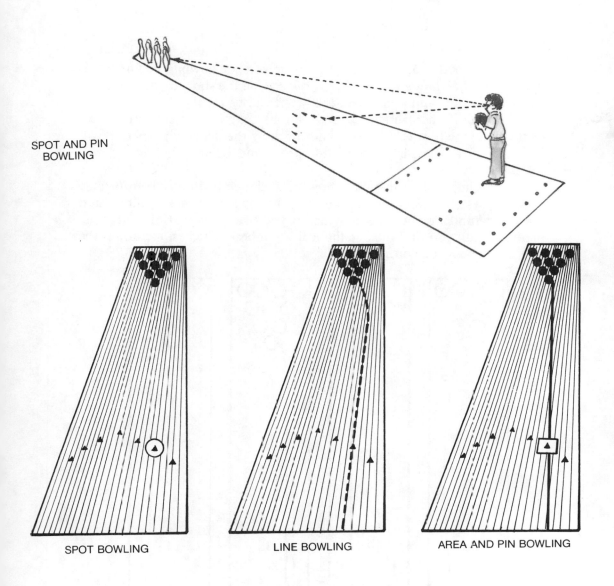

SPOT AND PIN
BOWLING

SPOT BOWLING   LINE BOWLING   AREA AND PIN BOWLING

Line bowling is a combination of spot and pin bowling. The idea is to select a starting spot, another spot at the foul line or thereabouts, and a spot out on the lane, giving you a line to your target. There are many variations because bowlers can draw their own target lines on the basis of what is easiest to hit and most comfortable for their physical and mental makeup.

Area bowling means giving yourself a larger area to hit. Instead of a strict one-arrow or one-board target, you settle for a little extra on each side with the arrow or the board as your main target. This tends to loosen up a bowler.

33

Most better bowlers use some form of spot bowling or line bowling. In spot bowling you must keep your eye on the spot so you can tell if you hit it or not and then make the proper adjustments.

It cannot be overemphasized that all targeting systems are dependent on the the bowler's starting and finishing the delivery properly, rolling the ball at the same angle and speed, and being consistent in ball release.

It is important that young bowlers find their own most comfortable targeting system. Every top pro has his or her own little tricks built around the basic fundamentals. So it is up to you to try the various targeting methods until you find the one that suits you best. The best method is the one that works for you.

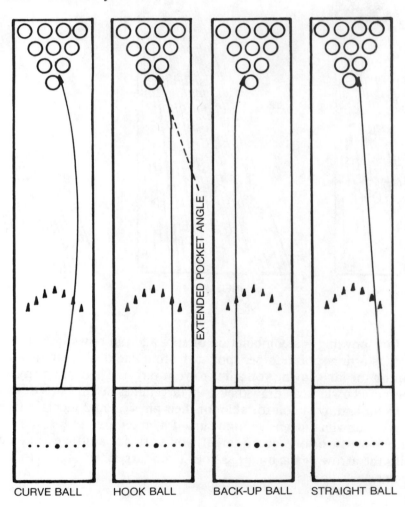

CURVE BALL   HOOK BALL   BACK-UP BALL   STRAIGHT BALL

7 | STRIKES, SPARES, AND SPLITS

A strike is the best single effort you can make in the sport of bowling. And oddly, a five-year-old or an eighty-year-old can come up with as perfect a strike as the world's greatest pros.

The strike comes easiest when the ball hits full into the 1–3 pocket at the proper angle, roughly on the seventeenth board. But the ball, even on a perfect hit, needs plenty of help in the way of pinfall. Regardless of the weight of the ball or the angle, there is deflection when the ball contacts the pins. They fall, but not before they push the ball off to the right, near the number 9 or 10 pin.

Let's say the ball knocks down only the one, three, five, and nine pins. The one hits the two, which hits the four, which hits the seven. In the same way, the three takes out the six, and the six fells the ten. The five is pushed into the eight to complete the chain reaction. Pins can fly up or go around one another, and this accounts for some odd leaves.

The name of the game in bowling is to hit the pocket as much as possible, and the number one pin, or headpin, is the key. Accuracy is more important than developing a powerful working ball, particularly for younger bowlers. If you are constantly near the pocket the strikes will come, and just as important, when you fail to strike, the spare leaves will be the less difficult ones.

No matter how good a strike bowler you are, and some pros roll as many as eight strikes a game, your score will suffer drastically if you can't make spares. Even if you come up with two or three strikes a game, making those spares can make you a highly respected bowler with a better-than-average score.

From the foul line the pins look as though they're bunched together closely, but they are a foot apart from center to center, and though the bowling ball seems big, it isn't nearly as big as it looks when it goes after the pins.

Most fans are amazed at how well the pros seem to make their spares. However, the fact is that they must contend with only about a third of the spares the average bowler must make, and most of their spares are single pins. There is no such thing as an easy spare, and the minute you lose your concentration is the minute you lose the spare.

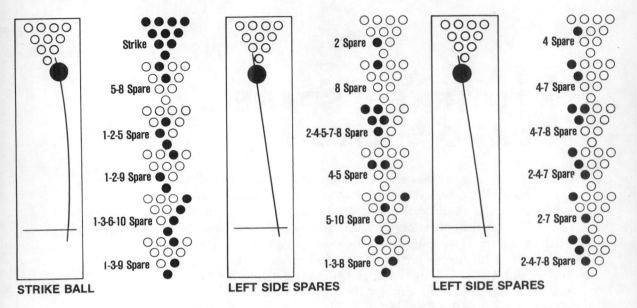

STRIKE BALL   **LEFT SIDE SPARES**   **LEFT SIDE SPARES**

All pros and instructors agree that there are a few keys to converting spares.

First, hit every pin with the ball, if possible.

Second, give yourself the best possible angle. The basic angles for spare shooting are your normal strike ball for middle-lane spares, left to right for ten-pin-area spares, and right to left for seven-pin-area spares. Always use as much of the lane as possible. Try to find yourself a pocket shot in the spare leave so you can attempt to roll your normal first ball.

For instance, on the difficult 2-4-5-8, known as the *bucket*, you should hit the 2-5 as though it were the 1-3 pocket. The two takes out the four, and the ball continues through to take the eight.

Always look for a key pin in any setup, such as the hidden pin of a double wood (one pin directly behind another) leave, the four pin in the 1-2-4, and the eight pin in the 1-2-8. On most spares the key pin will usually be the pin closest to you.

Sometimes the key pin is an imaginary pin. On the 4-5 split the key is the two pin that isn't there. On the 3-10 it's again an imaginary two pin. With each spare leave, the first thing you should do is determine the key pin that must be hit. Then decide where to hit it, the approach position, and the target.

Usually a one-board change on the approach will result in a three-board change at the finish. Remember, a lane is made up of individual boards, each about an inch in width. If you move one board toward the middle on the approach, the ball will wind up three boards to the right when it contacts the pins. If you move to the right one board, then the ball

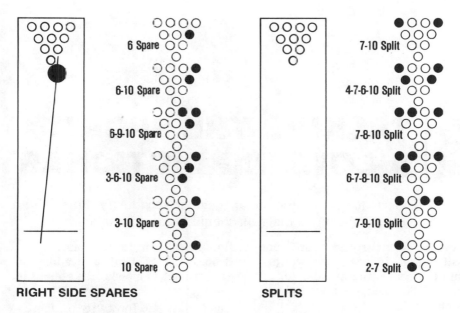

RIGHT SIDE SPARES

6 Spare
6-10 Spare
6-9-10 Spare
3-6-10 Spare
3-10 Spare
10 Spare

SPLITS

7-10 Split
4-7-6-10 Split
7-8-10 Split
6-7-8-10 Split
7-9-10 Split
2-7 Split

will finish three boards to the left when it finishes.

On all spares face your target. Draw an imaginary foul line, then square yourself to the new line as you would for a strike attempt. Watch other bowlers as they roll at spares so you can learn more about how the lane reacts.

There are 1,023 different possible spare leaves. Don't take any one of them for granted, but don't let them scare you either.

Splits are spare leaves too, and here you must use common sense. The almost impossible splits, the 4–6, 8–10, 7–10, and 4–6–7–10, are so rarely made that it makes sense to be sure of the one or two pins you can make, rather than to try to convert the spare since they are made only by some odd stroke of luck when pins bounce in ways they are not supposed to bounce.

This is not true of the baby splits, the 3–10 or 2–7 which are easiest to make, and the 5–7, 5–10, 4–7–10, and 6–7–10. They vary in difficulty, but all can and are made, as are the 4–5, 5–6, 7–8, and 9–10, all calling for the ball to be fit between two pins.

Bowling is full of numbers. Think numbers when you think spares. If you can make one extra spare each three games, your average will rise more than four points. And if you can make one more spare each game, your average will soar about eleven points. So it pays to study spare angles and the spare-making game plan best for you. After a time you should be able to automatically set up for almost any spare you leave without too much extra thought.

8 | TALKING THE SPORT: A BOWLING DICTIONARY

All sports have their special language or vocabulary. So it is with bowling. Here are the terms that you should become familiar with.

All-events: Games rolled in different classifications in the same tournament. Generally, the grand total of pins scored in team, doubles, and singles play.

Alley: An individual lane, also a bowling center.

Anchor: The final player in a lineup.

Approach: The physical area behind the foul line. Same as runway. Also the general name for a player's style of getting to the foul line.

Arrows: Targets or aiming guides embedded in the lane.

Baby split: The 3–10 or 2–7 spare leaves.

Bed: Another name for a single lane.

Bedposts: The 7–10 split.

Belly: To roll the ball in a wide arc, starting from the center of the lane. Also, the widest part of a bowling pin.

Blind: A score allowed a team to make up for a player's absence, usually based on the average of the missing bowler or predetermined by league or tournament rules.

Block: The illegal use of dressing on a lane to help steer the ball.

Blow: A missed spare.

Boards: The individual pieces of lumber used to construct a lane.

Box: Another name for frame.

Brooklyn: The left of the headpin for a right-handed bowler, the opposite for a lefty.

Channel: Name for gutter or depressions on either side of lane.

Cherry: Chopping off the front pin when two or more are standing.

Clean game: A game with a strike or spare in each of the frames.

Count: The number of pins downed on a ball, particularly important when a bowler is working on a spare or double strike.

Cranker: Bowler who utilizes a wide, sweeping hook ball.

Cushion: Padding in pit area to absorb impact of ball and pins.

Dead wood: Pins knocked down but remaining on lane or in channel. Must be removed before play can continue.

Deuce: The coveted 200 game or 200 average.

Dodo: An illegal bowling ball, either over regulation weight or not balanced properly.

Double: Two strikes in a row.

Double pinochle: The 4–6–7–10 split, also known as *big four, big ears.*

Double wood: Pins directly behind one another, 2–8, 3–9, 1–5.

Dovetails: Part of lane where maple and pine boards meet, also called *splice*.

Dutch 200: An even 200 game achieved by alternating strikes and spares.

Emblem: The design or logo on a bowling ball.

Error: A missed spare.

Fill: Pins knocked down when working on a spare or a double strike.

Foul: Going beyond the foul line with the hand or foot touching the playing surface.

Foul line: Black marking designating the separation of approach and lane.

Frame: The division of the game. Ten frames constitute a game.

Greek church: The 4-6-7-8-10 or 4-6-7-9-10 splits.

Handicap: Pins (points) awarded to lower-than-average scorer to equalize competition.

Heads: The portion of the lane from the foul line to approximately ten feet down the lane.

High hit: When the ball contacts the pin near its center. The term is usually used in reference to a ball hitting full into the number one or headpin.

Hole: Another name for the strike pocket, also another name for a split.

House ball: Bowling ball provided free by the bowling center.

Inside: A starting point near or to the left of center for a right-hander, the opposite for lefties.

Jersey: To the left of target for right-handers, to the right of target for lefties.

Leadoff: First player to roll in a team lineup.

Lift: Upward motion with flats of fingers at point of ball release.

Line: The path of a bowling ball. Also in many areas another name for a single game of bowling.

Maples: Bowling pins.

Mark: A strike or spare.

Match play: Tournament action in which bowlers roll against one another and receive bonus pins for winning.

Medal play: Action in which only total pinfall counts, no match play.

Miss: An error or blow.

Mixer: A rolled bowling ball with enough action on it to cause the pins to spin and bounce when hit.

Nose hit: A ball hitting full on the headpin.

One in the dark: The back pin in the 1-5, 2-8, or 3-9 spare.

Open: A frame in which a bowler does not register a strike or a spare.

Outside: A targeting angle starting close to the corner of the lane.

Perfect game: Score of 300. Twelve strikes in a row.

Pit: Area at end of lane to catch pins and ball.

Pitch: Angle at which a bowling ball hole is drilled.

Pocket: The strike zone, 1-3 for righties, 1-2 for lefties.

Poodle: A gutter or channel ball.

Railroad: A split.

Rap: When a pin remains standing on what seemed to be a perfect hit. Same as a tap.

Revolutions: The number of turns the ball takes to go from foul line to pins.

Sanctioned: Rolling in competition in accordance with ABC, WIBC, and YABA rules.

Sandbagger: Bowler who keeps average down purposely in order to receive a higher handicap.

Scratch: Actual score, no handicap.

Sleeper: A pin hidden behind another pin.

Slots: High-scoring lanes.

Sour apple: Weak-hitting ball.

Span: Distance from thumb hole to finger holes.

Spare: All pins downed with two balls.

Split: A spare leave in which the headpin is down and in order to make the spare, one pin must be sent to hit another (as in the 6–7) or the ball must be fitted between two pins (as in the 5–6).

Spot: Target on lane.

Strike: Knocking all ten pins down on the first ball of a frame.

String: A number of strikes in a row, usually three or more.

Track: The area most used on a lane, creating an invisible path to the pins. Also the area on a bowling ball where it rolls.

Turkey: Three strikes in a row.

Turn: Motion of the hand to apply action and direction at ball release.

Vent: A tiny hole drilled to relieve suction in finger holes.

Washout: The 1–2–10, 1–2–4–10, and varieties of same. A common spare leave, not a split, occurs when ball rolls in behind headpin.

✕ : Symbol for strike.

Important Abbreviations

ABC: American Bowling Congress.

AWBA: American Wheelchair Bowling Association.

BBIA: Billiard & Bowling Institute of America.

BPAA: Bowling Proprietors' Association of America.

BWAA: Bowling Writers Association of America.

FIQ: Fédération International des Quilleurs.

LPBT: Ladies Professional Bowlers Tour.

NBC: National Bowling Council.

NWBW: National Women Bowling Writers Association.

PBA: Professional Bowlers Association.

WIBC: Women's International Bowling Congress.

WBW: World Bowling Writers.

YABA: Young American Bowling Alliance.

9 | TIPS FROM TOP PROS

The professional bowlers listed here collectively have won every major title in bowling and millions of dollars in prize money and have appeared on national television hundreds of times. Many started as junior bowlers, and all give their time freely to help bowlers of all ages.

Donna Adamek: "Just remember, straight and slow, straight and slow as you go to the line. Always make sure you're lined up properly, and always take enough time, never rush any part of your game. And don't be discouraged when you're rolling poorly. It's a game of ups and downs. If you don't learn to take the downs, and it's not easy, you'll seldom enjoy the ups."

Earl Anthony: "Bowling is simply a sport of coordination and concentration, but always try to learn what you don't know. There is no defense in bowling. Don't throw the ball harder when you're mad, because it won't help, and it does no good to kick something. The best way to get better is to bowl against better bowlers. It teaches you to bowl under pressure because you must. The pressure on the pro tour doesn't come from the big money at stake, it comes from the competition."

EARL ANTHONY

Mike Aulby: "Most young bowlers try to turn the ball too early, and in their eagerness to put action on the ball, they lose it. Stay behind the ball and don't apply lift and turn until the point of release."

Patty Costello: "Your bowling ball almost becomes a part of you when you bowl. Treat it as you would other parts of yourself."

MIKE AULBY

Dave Davis: "I'm tall and thin, and tall bowlers have a tendency to tip forward at the start, so I lean a bit backwards and that helps prevent the tipping-over effect. Nothing beats practice, hard work, and, most of all, patience. Every bowler can string strikes, but the champions are the bowlers who always manage to squeeze an extra pin or two out of each game by that patience."

DAVE DAVIS

Gary Dickinson: "Don't try to kill the pins. Excess speed hurts more than it helps in most cases."

Mike Durbin: "Because bowling is a constantly changing game, year to year, week to week, and even game to game, try not to have too many ideas set in stone in your mind. Don't be afraid to make changes in your approach or delivery so long as you are fairly sure of yourself and it isn't a drastic switch from your normal, natural style."

MIKE DURBIN

Frank Ellenberg: "When you're fit you bowl better, and it doesn't take much to stay fit. A little regular walking, running, swimming, or cycling will do it. They keep your legs in shape, and legs are important in bowling. The wrist is also vital in bowling, so to develop a firmer and stronger wrist just squeeze a tennis ball several times a day when you're sitting around or watching TV."

DOTTY FOTHERGILL

Dotty Fothergill: "From the time you start bowling you should be aware of bowling under pressure because it is a natural part of the sport. In practice I make believe every ball means thousands of dollars, and when the ball does mean big money or a big title, I pretend it is only practice. Dream up your own method."

Nikki Gianulias: "No matter where you bowl, one of the best ways to get a line on how best to shoot spares is to watch the bowlers who roll before you do, then use your own experience and judgment to decide what's best for you. Don't ever take any spare for granted or consider any spare an easy spare. Some are just easier than others. And it really is true that if you make your spares, the strikes will come."

Steve Martin: "As a pro, making money is certainly important to me. But there's a million ways to make money, yet only a few ways to gain recognition and respect, and bowling is one of them."

STEVE MARTIN

Dick Ritger: "Carefully note what your ball does on every shot, and what happens when you make an adjustment."

Mark Roth: "Don't try to hook the ball too much. Work on a good, straight arm swing, close to the body. Pick an exact spot on the lane, but don't worry if you miss it by a little on either side. It will still be a good ball. And don't rush into heavier-weight bowling balls too quickly. Make sure you're ready by testing various weights first."

DICK RITGER

10 | PRACTICE, PRACTICE, PRACTICE!

A regular schedule of practice will improve any bowler, but *how* you practice is as important as *how much* you practice. Pinpoint the parts of your game where you feel you need help. Bowl alone for better concentration.

The scores you roll in practice are not important. You're looking to improve your game to the point where the big scores will always come, so practice is simply hard work, not an ego trip.

If possible, shadow bowl at times. That means to bowl without the pins up. That way you can concentrate more on your approach, your target areas on the lane, and your ball release.

Practice time is the time to try new equipment and new techniques, and no better method has been invented than that of trial-and-error. What looks fine when performed by a pro bowler can often be an impossibility for almost anyone else. Take your game apart and see what you're doing well, and where you're weak. Look in the mirror, check with teammates, fellow bowlers, and look for qualified helpers. Then put it all together.

You can practice at home. Practice your approach, your arm swing. Use an iron or a similar object as the ball and go over your movements again and again. If you have a large mirror to practice in front of, all the better. And some member of your family may even have a video camera to take pictures to show you how you look. Even still pictures can help.

Don't have half a dozen instructors. Select someone you have confidence in and listen to that person, whether it be a pro, a family member, or a friendly junior coach or bowler.

If you're working on a limited budget, and most young bowlers are, use it wisely. Don't blow all your practice time in one session. Shop for bargains. Many bowling centers offer special rates on off hours.

Roll as many different times as you can, because this will give you experience in varying lane conditions. If you want to try something different that you saw, heard, or read about or that you feel you might be comfortable with, try it. Don't worry how you might look. That's what practice is all about.

The mental side of bowling is very important. Most pros consider it the most vital part of any game. So, end each practice session with a strike, even if it does cost you for a few extra frames. It will leave you eager, happy, and full of confidence as you anticipate your next practice outing.

THE FINAL FRAME: THIS AND THAT

Etiquette

If you forget every rule of etiquette in bowling, do your best to remember the most important one: the use of plain old common sense.

A bowling center is your home away from home for a few hours, in many ways your own private country club. You wouldn't stomp spilled food or drink on your living room rug or place chewing gum under your dining room chairs, would you?

Respect the equipment, the various machinery, and the furniture that the bowling center attempts to keep in top shape for your enjoyment and that of other bowlers. Never use anyone's bowling ball or shoes unless you have permission to do so.

Be on time for your bowling league or tournament play. A team needs each individual working together, so when you're bowling well, try to lift a teammate who is rolling badly, and when you're rolling poorly, depend on them.

Be ready to bowl when it is your turn. Don't be off somewhere watching TV or talking to someone. When two bowlers are ready to roll at the same time, the bowler on the right has the right of way.

Confine your bowling to your lane. If you run or jump to another lane you may run into another bowler in the midst of his or her swing, and bowling balls can do damage.

Ask for instruction from anyone you feel might be helpful. Don't offer instruction unless asked.

Know the basic rules, available from the bowling center or from a junior bowling official.

Don't use foreign substances such as powder or chalk on your ball, shoes, or the approach, because they may damage the approach or cause problems for other bowlers. And don't try to fix any equipment that may break down. Leave that to the experts.

Bowling is a sport of deep concentration, so when another bowler is set and ready to go, don't talk to or heckle him or her. Bowling is a fun game, even in competition, and though there's a place for a zinger or two, loud griping and coarse language are out of place, and so are the ones who resort to such action.

You don't have to like losing. Indeed, you should dislike it, but since there will always be more losers than winners, you must learn to accept losing as the experience needed to become a winner. Accept winning and losing in a gracious manner.

Television

Bowling has long been one of the most popular features on network television. Local shows abound, too, featuring top pros, amateurs, men, women, mixed couples, and junior bowlers.

The pro tour telecasts are worth looking at for any young bowler. You can see how the pros do it. Don't try to copy exactly what they do, but try to select parts of their game that can fit in with your game. You can also learn much about how they play lanes, adjust, shoot spares, and concentrate.

The instant replays can be the biggest boon to a viewer. You can see how the pins fall, why they don't fall, what happens on a perfect hit, the effect of ball deflection, and almost everything else at one time or another.

So make it a point to watch any bowling TV show you can.

Competition

Once you get the feel of the sport, join a league as soon as possible. There are leagues for junior bowlers at every bowling center, and usually a wide choice of team play, from as few as two on a team to as many as five. Many centers also feature adult–junior leagues. Rolling in a league will teach you discipline and how to get along with others, and, since most leagues have certified coaches, the leagues will give you a chance to learn quickly. There are also many types of awards.

It doesn't matter what you average, since most leagues are handicapped, thus bringing every team to an almost even status. *An example of handicapping:* If one bowler averages 130 and the opponent 160, the lower-average bowler would have 30 pins added to his actual score for each game rolled.

Once into league play you will also want to roll in tournament competition. In every area there are bowling centers, city and state tournaments, and more and more national events for young bowlers. Most high schools field varsity teams, and more and more colleges are into bowling, both on an intramural basis and in intercollegiate competition.

Even if you excel as a junior bowler and seem ready to join adult leagues and get into money competition, stay a junior as long as possible. There is always plenty of time for that, and once you go out of the junior ranks there is no return.

Rules

Though bowling has many rules, there are a few judgment calls needed by officials. League rules can vary because leagues have the right to set certain standards of their own, such as amount of handicap, blind scores, rules regarding substitutes, tardiness, and various prizes and awards. Study the official rule book and the league rules. An informed bowler is a better bowler.

Strategy and Psychology

Since bowling is a sport with no defense, it becomes much more of a mental sport. There is little in the way of strategic moves, except in team play, where the placement of different players can be very important. For example, the leadoff or first bowler should be your peppiest bowler, the one who can start a rally. The anchor or final bowler should be your steadiest and most dependable bowler, not necessarily your best, but one who can roll a good ball in the clutch. Wanting to win and doing your best to win are the most important things in bowling and life. You will win and you will lose, and you will experience happiness and heartbreak. And in the long run, win or lose, you will be a winner.

Bowling: An Individual Sport

Once you get into bowling you will find that even in the basics there are some contradictions, and when you watch the top stars you will find that they will violate some of the basic rules.

All that indicates is that each person is an individual with his or her own character and traits. So if you can't do things exactly the way you'd like to or the way the book tells you, do your best within your own makeup. Basics are *guides*, the foundation upon which you can build, if necessary, in your own way.

Bowlers love to talk, and when they talk about their scores it is often said that they don't exaggerate, they just happen to remember big. Let's hope that your scores are so good you never have to remember big.

INDEX